Technology All Around Us

Robots

Clive Gifford

A^+

Smart Apple Media

First published in 2005 by Franklin Watts
96 Leonard Street, London EC2A 4XD

Franklin Watts Australia
Level 17/207 Kent Street, Sydney NSW 2000

Produced by Arcturus Publishing Ltd.
26/27 Bickels Yard, 151–153 Bermondsey Street, London SE1 3HA

Series concept: Alex Woolf, Editor: Alex Woolf, Designer: Simon
Borrough, Picture researcher: Glass Onion Pictures

Picture Credits
Science Photo Library: 4 (Peter Menzel), 5 (Peter Menzel), 6 (Sheila Terry),
7 (Maximilian Stock Ltd), 8 and cover (Sam Ogden), 9 (Peter Menzel),
10 (NASA / Carnegie Mellon University), 11 (Peter Menzel), 12
(James King-Holmes), 13 (Peter Menzel), 14 (Peter Menzel), 15 (Pascal
Goetgheluck), 16 (Alexis Rosenfeld), 17 (Peter Menzel), 18 (Alexis Rosenfeld),
19 (Peter Menzel), 20 (NASA), 21 (NASA), 22 (Peter Yates),
23 (Peter Menzel), 24 (Philippe Psaila), 25 (Lawrence Livermore National
Laboratory), 26 (Peter Menzel), 27 (Peter Menzel), 28 (Victor Habbick
Visions), 29 (Eye of Science).

Published in the United States by Smart Apple Media
2140 Howard Drive West, North Mankato, Minnesota 56003

Library of Congress Cataloging-in-Publication Data

Gifford, Clive.
Robots / by Clive Gifford.
p. cm. — (Technology all around us)
Includes bibliographical references and index.
ISBN 1-58340-752-9
1. Robotics—Juvenile literature. 2. Robots—Juvenile literature. I. Title. II.
Series.

TJ211.G48 2005
629.8'92—dc22   2004059014

9 8 7 6 5 4 3 2 1

Contents

Robots are an exciting and useful type of machine, and their impact on our world is increasing. Robots can perform a range of helpful tasks with little or no supervision by people.

Robots that can work completely by themselves are called autonomous. Others are remote-controlled by humans and are called teleoperated machines.

A researcher experiments with *Genghis*, a robot insect able to make simple decisions and respond to its environment.

Under Orders

Robots follow sets of instructions usually written as computer programs. Many robots can have their programs changed in order to perform different tasks.

The *Cye* home robot, for example, can fetch and carry items, act as a home security guard, or vacuum a room using different programs and attachments.

>> Looking Forward

The Thinking Robot
Robots can react to their environments and remember things. But their brains are nowhere near as flexible or powerful as the human brain. The goal of many people working in the field of artificial intelligence (AI) is to change that. Robots that can learn from their mistakes have already been created.

Sensors And Controllers

To work on their own, robots need to know information about themselves and the world around them. Devices called sensors collect information, such as the robot's position or the size of an obstacle ahead.

Sensors pass this data back to a robot's controller. This is the "brain" of the robot, which makes decisions and instructs a robot's parts. The controller is usually some form of computer microprocessor.

The Honda *P3* is a humanoid robot (see pages 8–9) capable of walking around obstacles in its path, as well as climbing down a flight of stairs without losing its balance.

Degrees Of Freedom

The moving parts of a robot are powered by actuators. These can be electric motors, hydraulic pistons, or compressed air systems.

Each direction in which a robot, or a robot part, can move is called a degree of freedom. Robot arms, for instance, are fitted with joints. Each joint may give a robot an extra degree of freedom.

What's In A Name? The word *robot* comes from the Czech word *robota*, meaning "forced labor." It was first used by Czech playwright Karel Capek in his 1920 play *Rossum's Universal Robots*.

Capek's play was about human-like robots that took over the world. This view of robots and their threat to people has remained a popular theme in sci-fi books and films ever since.

5

More than a million robots are at work today. Almost three-quarters of them are found in industry, where they perform tasks such as welding, spray painting, handling or sorting materials, and transporting items around a factory.

Never tiring or complaining, robots perform jobs that are difficult, unpleasant, or tedious for people. They also perform work beyond people's abilities, such as handling red-hot metal or drilling hundreds of small holes with perfect precision.

A pair of industrial AGVs transport barrels of oil around a factory floor without a human in sight.

Technology in Action

Skywash

It is 1996, and the staff at the German airline Lufthansa looks on in awe as a monstrous machine cleans airliners in record time. Called the *Skywash SW33*, the giant robot's arm measures 108 feet (33 m) in length and weighs more than 22 tons (20 t).

When it is cleaning a Boeing 747 jumbo jet, its brushes travel 2.4 miles (3.8 km). Traditional cleaning takes nine hours, but with *Skywash*, the job is done in just three and a half hours and uses half the water.

Automated Guided Vehicles (AGVs)

AGVs are mobile robots that work mainly in factories but are also found in hospitals and offices. They carry materials, supplies, and equipment around the workplace without a human driver.

Many of these wheeled machines use light sensors to follow a bright line on the floor.

The First Industrial Robot George Devol and Joseph Engelberger met at a party in 1956 and discussed sci-fi books and movies. Within five years, the pair had turned science fiction into fact with the world's first industrial robot, called the *Unimate I.*

This 4.4-ton (4 t) robot was employed at a General Motors car factory in the United States. Obeying step-by-step instructions recorded on a magnetic drum, the robot slowly but surely handled hot metal castings.

Demolition Robots

Robots are used in demolition, particularly in tight spaces where high dust levels and falling material could harm human workers.

The *Brokk 40* robot arm can be fitted with tile-chiseling and concrete-crushing tools. It can perform demolition work four times faster than a team of human workers.

A robot arm guides a welding torch into perfect position. It is directed with unerring accuracy by a system of lasers and miniature cameras.

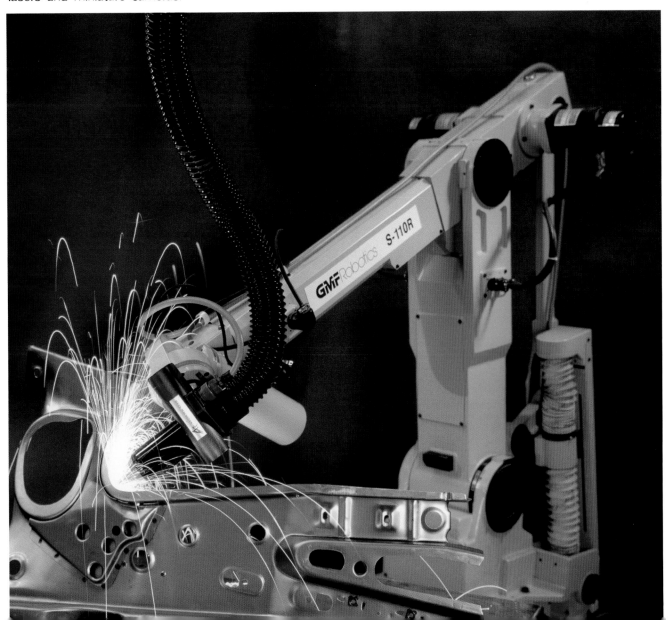

Humanoid Robots

For centuries, people have been fascinated by the idea of creating machines that look and act like themselves. Mechanical models of people, moved by clockwork, appeared in medieval clocks and are called automata.

Today, humanoid robots look and act like people. They are also capable of reacting to their environments and making decisions.

Robotics researcher Cynthia Breazeal plays with *Kismet*. This robot has been equipped with sensors and software that simulate the behavior of a baby or young child.

Balancing Bipeds

Early biped (two-legged) robots struggled to keep their balance, especially when walking. This is because they did not have the sophisticated balancing system found in the human ear and brain.

Advances in robotics have led to robots, such as the Honda *Asimo*, being able to walk and even climb stairs.

>> Looking Forward

Giving Robots Personality Robotics teams in many countries are seeking to build robots that can display emotions and develop their own personalities.

In the U.S., a robot baby called *Robota* is being built that watches human actions and learns to imitate them in order to develop different ways of acting.

Another robot called *Kismet* is able to show a range of emotions as different facial expressions, using actuators to move various parts of its face.

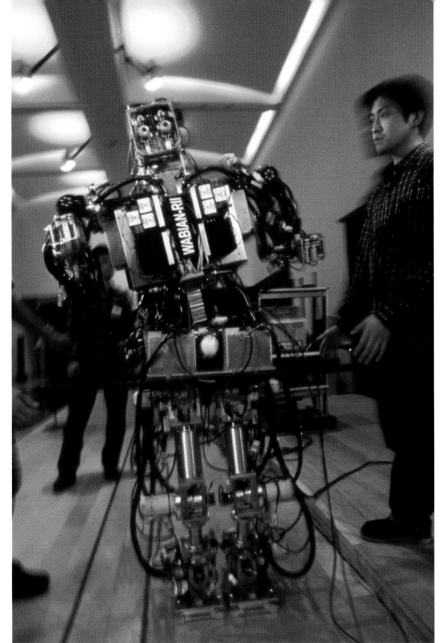

Researchers look on as Waseda University's *WABIAN II* humanoid robot walks through a Japanese laboratory.

Sony *Qrio*

The Sony *Qrio* is a humanoid robot, just 28 inches (58 cm) tall, that can walk, dance, and speak a vocabulary of 60,000 words. Using microphones and digital cameras, the *Qrio* can recognize voices and faces, and read e-mail and Web pages.

Gripping Stuff

Some humanoid robots strive to equal a human being's ability to hold and manipulate objects of different sizes, shapes, and weights.

COG, for example, has four-fingered hands covered in a touch-sensitive material. The fingers can tell the robot what sort of material they are gripping. The robot can adjust the force of its grip to prevent an object from slipping. It can also release some pressure to keep from damaging the object.

 Looking
Back

Made In Japan Between 1980 and 1984, Waseda University developed a pioneering humanoid robot called *WABOT-2*. Although it could not balance or walk, *WABOT-2* wowed the world with its impressive musical abilities.

The robot's cameras and controller enabled *WABOT-2* to read a piece of sheet music and play the music on an electric organ with its two robot hands.

Robots can explore places where people cannot or dare not go. These include places too far away or simply too dangerous for people to reach.

Robot explorers don't need to carry food, water, or other supplies. Energy to power their parts can come from batteries or solar panels. Robots can be built with their electronic components protected so that they can work in boiling-hot or freezing-cold environments.

Looking Back

The Inferno In July 1994, an eight-legged robot called *Dante II* climbed slowly into the mouth of an active volcanic crater on Mount Spurr, Alaska. Despite being hit by a boulder that damaged one of its legs, *Dante II* managed to reach the crater floor.

It collected video footage using its eight cameras and took samples of gases and water found in the crater. But a fall ended the robot's mission, and it had to be airlifted out by helicopter.

Dante II in action exploring Mount Spurr. The robot was equipped with sensors that measured the sorts of gases found in the volcano.

Professor William "Red" Whittaker with *Nomad*. The robot has trekked in the hot, dry deserts of Chile and traversed freezing Antarctica.

Exploring Ancient Egypt

Robots can explore cramped environments too small for humans to enter. In 2002, iRobot's *Pyramid Rover* traveled down a shaft just eight inches (20 cm) high and eight inches (20 cm) wide. The robot explored a place unseen by modern eyes—inside the 4,500-year-old ancient Egyptian Great Pyramid.

Industrial Explorers

Many robot explorers don't make the headlines but perform valuable work in industry. Long, narrow, snake-like robots, made up of many flexible sections, are sent down pipelines and sewer systems, where they check for leaks and other problems.

Other robots equipped with sniffing sensors can enter storage tanks to hunt for gas leaks.

Meteorite Hunter

It is January 2000. The location is the icy wastes of Antarctica, where the sub-zero temperatures would kill a person in a matter of hours. A chunky robot rover almost the size of a Volkswagen Beetle car is hunting for meteorites. Its name is *Nomad*.

Nomad covers an area of 26,900 square feet (2,500 sq m) over 10 days. It uses cameras and sensors to examine 100 different rocks. On January 22, *Nomad* discovers a meteorite, the first of five that the robot finds.

Service robots perform a range of dull and repetitive but useful tasks. Some can fill a car's gas tank, while others carry a golfer's bag of clubs. In Japan, robot shopping carts obediently follow customers around a department store.

Service robots are in their infancy, but many more are expected to appear in the near future.

The *Hefter Robot Cleaner* in action in Manchester Airport, England. The robot is guided by ultrasound sensors and lasers to avoid colliding with objects, and it issues a spoken message if people get in the way.

Clean Machine

Cleaning robots are used to scrub the floors in several British hospitals, on the Paris Metro, and at a number of airports in Asia. Climbing robots, designed in France and Germany, have scaled the sides of skyscrapers, cleaning windows.

Looking Forward

Robo-gardeners Delicate seedlings can now be repotted using special robot arms. Robot lawnmowers are already on sale to the public. Robots used to hunt down garden pests may also soon be a reality.

Slugbot is a small, four-wheeled prototype robot. It can capture 100 slugs per hour with its three-fingered claw. The slugs rot in a special refueling chamber. Gases from the rotting slugs are converted into electricity to power the robot.

Served By Service Bots

Robot waiters and bartenders are becoming a reality. In Yo Sushi restaurants in Europe, AGV robots (see page 6) move between tables carrying drinks to customers.

Cynthia is a resident bartender in London's Wicked Bar and Restaurant. She is a seven-foot (2 m) humanoid robot with two gripping arms that help her serve one of 75 different cocktails.

This prototype German robot can fill a vehicle's tank with gas with no supervision required.

Meet *Minerva*

It is 1998, and visitors arrive at the National Museum of American History in Washington, D.C. A squat, gray machine glides over to meet the visitors, welcoming them with words spoken in a soft, human-like voice.

The robot is named *Minerva,* and it guides visitors through the Material World exhibition at the museum. The robot plots its own path through the exhibition, speaking, singing, and answering questions via its touchscreen.

Get in its way once, and the robot stops and says "Excuse me" in polite tones. Get in its way repeatedly, and expect to get a blast of its horn and to see its face form a frown.

Robots can save lives. They can enter disaster zones or dangerous areas, seeking out victims or trying to stop a fire or chemical leak. Robots also perform the nuclear power industry's dirty work, helping to dismantle damaged nuclear power plants.

In the future, large groups of small, highly mobile machines may work together. Called a robot swarm, these robots would scour an area, searching for disaster victims.

Looking Forward

Treating Trapped Survivors The Center for Robot Assisted Search and Rescue (CRASAR) is building robots that can squeeze their way through a disaster site and reach trapped victims.

The robots will perform a medical diagnosis on patients, checking their vital signs. They will also bring the survivors water, oxygen, and basic medical supplies. The robots' radios will provide a communications link between the victims and rescue forces.

The Japanese *Blue Dragon* robot crawls over a pile of rubble using a nose-mounted digital camera to "see" what lies in its path.

Firefighters

Firefighting robots are currently being tried out. They can handle heat from a blaze better than human firefighters. They are also unaffected by lethal, poisonous smoke. Some can use regular firefighting tools such as hoses and extinguishers.

Expendable Machines

Robots are used to detect land mines or handle unexploded bombs without putting people at risk. Bomb-disposal robots usually move on wheels or tracks and are equipped with a robot arm. Different tools can be fitted to the arm. Sharp steel probes can be used to break windows. Grippers and claws can manipulate suspicious packages.

Some bomb-disposal robots are fitted with disrupters. These fire a powerful jet of water into a bomb to break up its circuits before the bomb can explode.

Technology in Action

Bomb Disposal in Israel
It is 2002, and the police are called to a bus stop near the Israeli city of Haifa. There are fears that an unconscious man is a suicide bomber carrying deadly explosives on his body.

The police deploy a tracked bomb-disposal robot. Controlled from a safe distance, the robot uses its manipulator arm to turn the man over. Cameras and sensors send data back to the bomb-disposal team. Finally, the all-clear is given, thanks to the robot.

A tracked bomb-disposal robot maneuvers a water-cannon disrupter into position to disarm the circuits of a car bomb.

Flying Robots

Most robots are fairly slow-moving on land or in water. Flying robots known as Unmanned Aerial Vehicles (UAVs) have to travel more rapidly. Their wings must move through the air fast enough to create the lift needed to keep them airborne. Because of their high speeds, almost all UAVs are remote-controlled.

Technology in Action

Round-the-World Robot

In April 2001, an aircraft unlike any other flew across the Pacific Ocean, from the U.S. to Australia. The machine had a wingspan of 115 feet (35 m) and was called *Global Hawk.* It was an unmanned aerial vehicle and the first flying robot to cross the Pacific.

Flying nonstop for 23 hours and 20 minutes, the robot completed its 8,078-mile (13,000 km) trip without a hitch. On later flights, it broke altitude and endurance world records for flying robots.

This unmanned aircraft is being prepared for flight. It will act as a flying target to test the accuracy of missiles at a French missile-testing center.

Spies in the Sky

A number of unmanned aerial vehicles are today being used as spies in the sky. Equipped with powerful zoom cameras, these robots can fly over enemy territory. Some fly at very high altitudes to avoid enemy aircraft or missiles. Others fly below enemy radar at low, ground-hugging altitudes.

One unusual flying spy is called *Cypher*. This U.S.-made, doughnut-shaped machine has helicopter-style blades that spin inside its body. This gives the robot the ability to hover in mid-air and maneuver between buildings.

Looking Forward

Tiny Fliers Micro Aerial Vehicles (MAVs) are tiny flying machines, often with wingspans of less than six inches (15 cm) and weighing less than four ounces (100 g).

In the future, squadrons of these machines may fly together performing tasks such as traffic monitoring, police surveillance, and search-and-rescue operations.

A robot helicopter hovers over a simulated dangerous chemicals spill. It can photograph and provide important information on a spill without risking the lives of human rescue workers.

Pest Controllers

The Japanese company Yamaha has produced a range of small robot helicopters that spray fields more efficiently than crop-dusting aircraft.

Yamaha's *RMAX* robot can spray 74 acres (30 ha) per day but flies closer to the ground and uses much less pesticide. This not only saves money but means that less harmful pesticide builds up in the soil or seeps into water supplies.

Another flying robot makes a novel pest controller at airports. *Robofalcon*, with its seven-foot (2 m) wingspan, looks like an oversized bird of prey and scares bird flocks from runways.

Diving puts people and machines under pressure. At depths deeper than 260 feet (80 m), humans cannot survive unless they are inside protective diving suits or submarines.

Robots make great underwater divers. They don't need large supplies of air and can be built to withstand great pressure. They can also travel for hours, or ever days, without surfacing.

RoboPike, a robotic fish, leaps out of the water. *RoboPike* has a series of flexible body parts controlled by electric motors, allowing it to mimic the swimming actions of a real fish.

Looking Back

AUSS One of the first AUVs was the *Advanced Unmanned Search System* (*AUSS*). It took 10 years to develop before its launch in 1983. The 16-foot (5 m), torpedo-shaped robot had no manipulator arm, and its heavy zinc battery packs took more than 20 hours to recharge.

In 1992, the long-serving robot discovered the wreckage of a 1950s *Douglas Skyraider* aircraft.

ROVs and AUVs

There are two main types of underwater robots—ROVs and AUVs. ROV stands for Remotely Operated Vehicle. These machines are controlled by a human operator, usually from a ship to which the robot is linked by a cable.

AUV stands for Autonomous Underwater Vehicle. These robots can navigate by themselves, although they may be pre-programmed to patrol a certain area or dive to a certain depth.

In 2003, the British-built *Autosub* AUV was programmed to travel more than 62 miles (100 km) underneath the ice shelves of Antarctica.

Surveying and Discovery

Underwater robots monitor the world's seas and oceans. They carry sensors that measure water temperature, pollution, and their effects on sea life.

When fitted with arms, grippers, and other tools, some robots can help recover wrecked aircrafts, ships, and submarines. In 1999, the *Deep Drone* ROV helped recover the flight recorder from an EgyptAir airliner that crashed in the Atlantic Ocean.

Technology in Action

This ROV robot is collecting 2,000-year-old jugs from the Mediterranean seabed.

The Deepest Dive Ever
Date: March 24, 1995. Location: Challenger Deep in the Pacific Ocean, the deepest place on Earth. The 16-foot (5 m) *Kaiko* robot travels deeper than any other robot, to a depth of 35,797 feet (10,911 m) below sea level.

The robot uses its powerful manipulator arm to place a plaque on the ocean floor. It powers up its lights and cameras to photograph marine life before beginning its slow climb back to the surface.

A robotic arm extends from the space shuttle *Endeavor* as it docks with the International Space Station.

Robots are often used in space exploration to perform one-way missions, when they have no chance of returning to Earth.

A number of robotic probes have flown past, or landed on, the planets of our solar system. The vast distances involved, and the extreme conditions on other planets, mean that it will likely remain easier to send machines instead of humans for many decades to come.

Exploring the Solar System

October 1998 saw the launch of the most intelligent spacecraft ever built: *Deep Space 1*. There were three AI systems on board, each with a different task:

● **The Autonomous Navigation System** steered the craft by comparing its position to well-known stars and asteroids.

● **The Remote Agent** was the spacecraft's "brain." It was programmed with a set of goals, but it had freedom, too. If it spotted an interesting asteroid or comet, for example, *Deep Space 1* could stop what it was doing and investigate.

● **The Beacon Monitor** was the spacecraft's communication system, transmitting messages back to Earth, such as "Everything's fine," or "I need help!"

Mars Milestone In 1976, the first robots to visit Mars landed safely. The *Viking I* and *Viking II* landers sent back the first high-resolution photos of the Martian surface.

Unlike later roving robots, the two *Vikings* were unable to move. A simple robot arm collected rock and soil samples close to the robots. These samples were analyzed inside the machines.

Robot Colonies Future Mars rovers are already being planned that will be able to adapt to different kinds of terrain.

The ultimate goal is to send teams of robot rovers to work together on the Martian surface. They would build robot colonies and lay the foundation for human visits and human bases.

Exploring The Red Planet

NASA's two Mars Exploration Rovers, *Spirit* and *Opportunity*, reached the red planet in January 2004. Over the course of their 90-day missions, the robots acted independently to navigate across parts of Mars.

The robots traveled up to 330 feet (100 m) per day. They investigated the planet's rocks and found strong evidence that water may once have existed on Mars.

A Mars Exploration Rover. Cameras mounted on its mast provide panoramic views of Mars. The robot arm (bottom left) carries further cameras, sensors, and a tool that can grind away the outer surface of a rock.

Robots can assist human surgeons in performing operations with incredible accuracy and without a hint of hand tremor. Some can drill pinpoint holes in bones. Others hold essential tools in place or transmit pictures from inside a patient's body.

Robots can help people with disabilities live a more normal life. A Japanese robot arm system called *Myspoon* helps people feed themselves without the aid of a nurse.

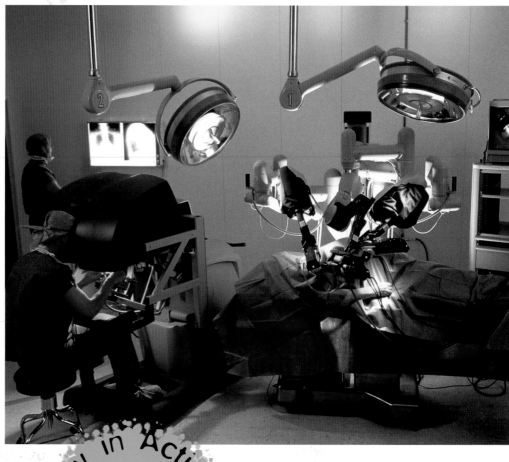

A human surgeon (bottom left) views an operation using 3D images while controlling the *Da Vinci* robot (center) during microsurgery.

Virtual Reality Operations

Robots sometimes enable surgeons to operate without having to touch the patient. Working from a separate room, the surgeon operates by looking at a "virtual reality" image of the patient.

The movements of the surgeon's hands are transmitted from the gloves he is wearing to a manipulator in the operating room.

Cutting Across Continents

It is June 2000. A patient at a hospital in Rome is having surgery on his kidneys. However, the surgeon performing the operation is not in the room, or even in the country. He is in Baltimore, Maryland.

Through a combination of computers, telecommunication, cameras, and an advanced surgical robot, the surgeon is able to see, touch, and manipulate as necessary to carry out a successful operation. The robot offers three-dimensional vision and a perfectly still hand.

Nursebots

Researchers are working to develop mobile personal service robots to help the elderly and other people who need regular supervision. Working in nursing homes or in people's own homes, the robots would remind patients when to take their medication and could fetch and carry items for them.

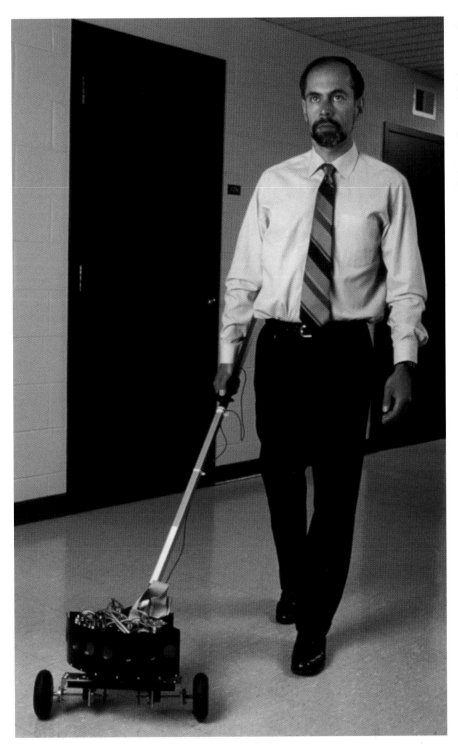

Rehab Robots Patients recovering from major accidents and operations can require hundreds of hours of physiotherapy.

Researchers in the U.S., Germany, Denmark, and Japan are developing rehab robots to help patients exercise. These robots will support patients' bodies while directing them to move in the safest and most beneficial way to improve their health.

Nursebots would be programmed to detect emergency situations such as heart failure and be able to alert emergency services. Eventually, these robots could become advanced enough to provide companionship for elderly people who live alone.

Guidecane, a robot guide for the blind, has a series of ultrasonic sensors that detect obstacles in its path. These are used to constantly update and recalculate the best route.

Today, robots are increasingly being used in military situations. Robots can act as spies or security guards, or check out potential threats and traps.

Robotic rifles, controlled from a distance of up to 1,100 yards (1 km), are under development. As more military robots enter service, the prospect of robot-led conflicts 30 or 40 years from now is not so far-fetched.

Robot Sentries

On the ground and under the water, robot sentries and security guards can patrol and keep watch with their sensors and camera systems. They can be stationed at the perimeters of a base or travel through the corridors of a building. Unlike human guards, robots remain alert and can work unceasingly for long shifts.

Robots In Iraq

A number of robots were deployed during the invasion of Iraq by U.S.-led coalition forces in 2003. Some were land robots such as *Packbot* and *Matilda*, sent to check out areas for booby traps and other threats. Most were UAVs (see pages 16–17) used to spy on targets or enemy troop movements.

One unit of soldiers was about to land in a secret location in Iraq when a *Predator* flying robot alerted the unit to dangers on the ground. The mission was aborted, probably saving some of the soldiers' lives.

This mobile wheeled robot, fitted with a protective frame, is designed to be sent into danger areas and report back on potential threats without risking human soldiers' lives.

Robotic Assassination

November 3, 2002. A *Predator* UAV flies over the Middle Eastern country of Yemen. It carries a deadly cargo—a Hellfire air-to-ground guided missile.

The robot flier is being controlled by a CIA pilot on the ground in the African nation of Djibouti. It homes in on its target—a vehicle carrying six members of the al-Qaeda terrorist group. The *Predator* releases the Hellfire missile, which destroys the vehicle and kills the terrorists inside it.

The *Raptor* UAV is designed to fly over battlefields and provide early warning of short-range missiles fired by the enemy.

Looking Back

ROBART In the early 1980s, the American ROBART project produced the first robot security guards capable of working by themselves. *ROBART 1* could only spot movement using its motion sensors. It could not assess whether the movement was a human intruder or not.

ROBART III, completed in 1993, was a vast improvement. The robot could detect and track an intruder.

25

A Japanese boy plays with his Sony *AIBO* robot dog. The *AIBO* mimics real dog actions such as barking and playing fetch and can also respond to its owner.

It is not all hard work for robots. Some provide people with great entertainment. Demonstration robots impress people at fairs and events, while the latest generation of home robots boast some amazing features.

Robot Pets and Toys

Robots at home can be excellent playmates. Many can speak and recognize hundreds or thousands of words, play games, make music, and perform simple tasks.

Sony's *AIBO* robot dog is the best-selling home robot. It is capable of interacting with owners and displaying six different emotions.

Looking Back

Early Hobby Bots Heathkit's *Hero-1* was a popular hobby robot of the early 1980s, despite costing more than $1,000. Owners had to slowly build its 15 circuit boards. The robot's arm could be programmed to lift objects that weighed less than a pound (440 g).

The robot had just four kilobytes of memory. Today, a typical home computer's hard drive has more than five million times as much memory space.

Sporting Robots

Fast-moving, dynamic ball sports can make ideal test applications for serious robotics research. They require a robot's sensors, controller, and movement systems to all work together quickly and accurately.

Toshiba has developed a two-armed robot that can play a simple game of volleyball, while the *Dynamic Brain* humanoid robot can juggle balls.

Robot Competitions

Dozens of competitions enable people to pit their robot-building and programming skills against others. Some are destructive robot combat competitions such as Battling Bots or Robot Wars, which first appeared in 1994. Others require robots to work together in a team to play a form of soccer in worldwide Robocup competitions.

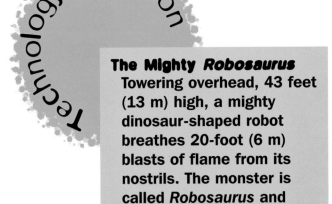

Technology in Action

The Mighty *Robosaurus*
Towering overhead, 43 feet (13 m) high, a mighty dinosaur-shaped robot breathes 20-foot (6 m) blasts of flame from its nostrils. The monster is called *Robosaurus* and entertains and amazes crowds at events.

Using its powerful hydraulic grippers, *Robosaurus* lifts cars, trucks, and even old aircraft up to the height of a five-story building. It then crushes them with more than 11 tons (10 t) of force.

Robosaurus shoots giant flames from its nostrils. This entertainment robot weighs a hefty 28.5 tons (26 t).

The robot revolution has barely begun. Robots are in their infancy, and many challenges lie ahead. No one can predict with certainty what future technology will bring, but advances are occurring every year.

The numbers of robots, the tasks they can perform, and their ability to assist people are all expected to increase dramatically. More and more robots are likely to serve in military and police forces and in hospitals, schools, and offices.

Disarming land mines is tough, slow, and dangerous work. In the future, flying mine-disposal robots may be able to clear land without risk.

Looking Back

Shakey Robots have made major strides forward since the arrival of the first robots in the 1960s. The first mobile robot was called *Shakey* and was the size of several people. Controlled by a computer that filled an entire room, the robot took around 30 minutes to move 3 feet (1 m)!

Today's machines are far quicker and more powerful than *Shakey*. And they can be made small enough to sit in the palm of your hand.

Home Helpers

In the future, it is likely that robots will perform a range of valuable tasks in the home. These multi-function machines will be able to play games, guard the house, and educate children and adults.

Such home robots will be capable of communicating with smart appliances in the kitchen and performing routine shopping and research tasks for their owners over the Internet.

Farther And Faster

As robots become safer, more reliable, and better at navigating, they will be built to travel and operate at faster speeds. Some may also travel to other galaxies across the universe.

Nanobots Technology is shrinking. A nanometer is a billionth of a meter—the width of 10 atoms. In the distant future, nanotechnology may be capable of building robots to this phenomenally small scale.

Their impact could be enormous. In medicine, nanobots could scrub blood vessels free of cholesterol and unblock clogged arteries and veins. Nanobots could inhabit materials and machinery, detecting wear and repairing damage.

Other space robots will land on and explore the planets and moons of our solar system. Launched in March 2004, the *Rosetta-Philae* robot probe hopes to ride piggyback on a comet in 2014 after a journey of more than 4.4 billion miles (7 billion km).

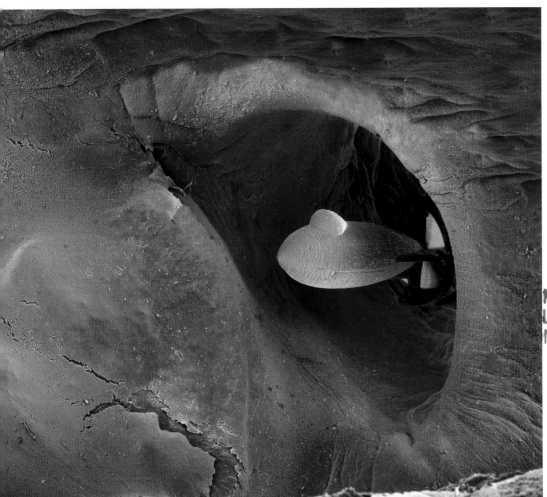

An artist's impression of what a nanobot submarine, designed to travel through a human blood vessel, might look like. Such a robot may be capable of removing cholesterol and reducing the chances of heart disease.

1921 Playwright Karel Capek is the first to coin the term "robot" in his play *Rossum's Universal Robots*.

1938 The first programmable spray-painting machine is designed for the DeVilbiss Company.

1940s The first computers, including *Colossus* and *ENIAC*, are invented and used.

1948 *Cybernetics*, a book by MIT professor Norbert Weiner, is published. The book looks at how communications and control work in animals and might work in machines.

1950s George Devol and Joseph Engelberger form the first company to develop and sell robots.

1959 The Artificial Intelligence Laboratory at MIT is founded.

1966 One of the earliest mobile robots, *Shakey*, is invented.

1969 The first computer-controlled robot arm, driven by electric motors and called the *Stanford Arm*, is invented.

1975 The *PUMA* robot arm is invented. Versions of this arm and its technology become widely used in industry.

1976 The robot arms on the *Viking I* and *II* spacecraft become the first robots to work on the surface of another planet (Mars).

1979 The *Stanford Cart* is developed. It is an autonomous robotic vehicle that can navigate across a room full of obstacles.

1980s The *WABOT* and *WABIAN* series of humanoid robots are developed at Waseda University, Japan.

1986 The Remotely Operated Vehicle *Jason Jr.* photographs the inside of the wreck of the *Titanic*.

1988 The first *Helpmate* AGV starts work carrying supplies around an American hospital.

1990 The *Robodoc* surgical assistant robot is invented and tested.

1994 The Robot Wars competition is founded.

1997 The first RoboCup football competition is held.

1997 *Sojourner* becomes the first robot to move around on the surface of another planet when it reaches Mars.

1998 Work begins on MIT's groundbreaking *Kismet* robot.

1999 The Sony corporation release its first *AIBO* robotic dogs.

2001 The *Global Hawk* UAV travels more than 8,125 miles (13,000 km) across the Pacific.

2002 Humanoid robots play soccer at RoboCup for the first time.

actuator A system or device, such as an electric motor, that makes part or all of a robot move.

automata Mechanical devices that imitate the movements of a person or another living creature.

autonomous Describing a machine that makes decisions and works by itself.

biped A two-legged creature or machine, such as a robot.

circuit board Boards containing electronic parts linked together.

compressed air system A way of moving a robot by using air in tubes to push its parts.

controller The part of the robot that makes decisions and instructs other parts of the robot.

degrees of freedom The different directions in which a robot can move.

feedback Information about a robot or its surroundings that is collected from sensors and sent to the robot's controller.

flight recorder A system housed in a tough box that records the speed, direction, and other important details of an aircraft flight.

humanoid A robot that resembles or acts like a human.

hydraulic pistons A piston is a sliding shaft that fits closely inside a tube called a cylinder. Hydraulic pistons are moved by liquid in a system to drive the parts of some robots.

hydraulics A power system using liquids in cylinders; it is used in some robots.

International Space Station A large spacecraft holding up to seven astronauts, which orbits Earth and is expected to be completed in 2006.

kilobyte A measure of computer memory. A regular floppy disk holds 1,440 kilobytes.

manipulator Another word for a robot gripper or tool that handles objects.

microprocessor A small computer built from one or a small number of silicon chips.

nanotechnology Technology created at an incredibly small scale measured in billionths of a meter.